About Me: Chris T. Risen

Hello and welcome! I'm Chris T. Risen, a seasoned professional with an extensive background in direct marketing, affiliate marketing, sales funnels, and leading dynamic sales teams. With years of invaluable experience under my belt, I've had the privilege of being a partner in one of the esteemed organizations recognized on the Inc 500 list of fastest-growing companies.

Professional Background

My journey in the dynamic field of marketing began over a decade ago, where my innate passion for connecting products with people found its true calling. Over the years, I have dedicated my skills and effort to marketing, where I've worked tirelessly to understand the intricacies and nuances that drive successful campaigns.

I've spearheaded marketing initiatives for eight distinctive brands, each with its unique identity, audience, and market position. This diversity in experience has not only broadened my perspective but also deepened my insights into the multifaceted world of marketing, making me adaptable and proficient in handling various marketing challenges and opportunities.

Expertise

Direct Marketing: With a robust background in direct marketing, I've developed and executed campaigns that directly engage the target audience, driving response and conversions through carefully crafted strategies and messages.

Affiliate Marketing: In the realm of affiliate marketing, I've worked on both sides of the spectrum—promoting products as an affiliate and driving sales through affiliates. This comprehensive experience has provided me with a deep understanding of the affiliate marketing landscape.

Sales Funnels: Mastering the art and science of sales funnels, I've successfully created and optimized conversion-focused funnels that not only attract but also retain customers, maximizing lifetime value and enhancing customer satisfaction.

Sales Teams: Leading high-performance sales teams has been one of my areas of expertise. By fostering a collaborative and motivated environment, I've guided teams to exceed sales targets while maintaining a focus on providing value to our clients and customers.

Inc 500 Fastest Growing Company Partnership: Being a partner in an Inc 500 recognized company has been a monumental milestone in my career. It is a testament to the collective hard work, innovation, and relentless pursuit of excellence that defines my approach to business and marketing.

My Approach

I approach marketing as a dynamic, evolving field that requires a blend of creativity, analytics, and an unerring focus on customer needs. In every campaign, strategy, or project I undertake, the customer is always at the core. By understanding their needs, preferences, and behaviors, I craft marketing strategies that resonate, engage, and convert.

Here's to successful marketing endeavors and the exciting journey that each campaign brings. Looking forward to crossing paths with like-minded professionals, collaborators, and enthusiasts in the field!

Chris T. Risen

Introduction

Welcome to "A Beginner's Guide to Starting a Home Business: Passive Income Made Simple"! Launching a home business might seem like a gigantic task, especially if you're a beginner. But don't worry! This book is your friendly and uncomplicated starting point. It's designed to gently walk you through the process of starting a business that earns money for you without requiring your constant attention.

Purpose of the Book

This book is a friendly primer for those who wish to understand and step into home entrepreneurship comfortably. It speaks in a language that is easy to grasp, introducing you to the essentials of planning, initiating, and growing a business right from your home. The aim is to provide you with a clear roadmap towards generating extra income without the confines and pressures of a traditional job, helping you inch closer to your dreams of financial stability and freedom.

Who Should Read This Book

- **Aspiring Entrepreneurs**: Individuals considering starting a business but are unsure where to begin or which business model to adopt will find invaluable insights and guidance in these pages.
- **Working Professionals:** If you are currently employed but seeking ways to earn additional income without significantly disrupting your career, this guide offers flexible options suited for busy schedules.
- **Stay-at-Home Parents**: For parents juggling household responsibilities and looking for convenient, home-based income-generating opportunities, this guide presents practical and feasible solutions.
- **Retirees:** If you're retired but wish to remain financially active and independent, the book provides business ideas and advice tailored to your unique needs and

experiences.

- **Students and Young Adults:** For those at the onset of their professional lives, this book serves as an introduction to the entrepreneurial world, presenting a foundation for building passive income streams early on.

If you see yourself in any of the above categories and are intrigued by the idea of earning from home with minimal daily effort, this book is written especially for you. It's time to turn the page and begin your delightful journey into the realm of home-based entrepreneurship!

Step 1: Understanding Passive Income

Introduction

As we embark on the journey of starting a home business focusing on passive income, it is pivotal to grasp the fundamental concept of what passive income truly is. This foundational step will navigate through its definition, benefits, and dispel common myths associated with passive income.

Definition of Passive Income

Passive income is money earned on a regular basis with minimal effort required to maintain it once the initial work has been completed. Unlike active income—where your earnings are directly tied to the hours you work—passive income is more resilient and flexible. Examples encompass earnings from rental property, dividends from investments, royalties from publishing a book, or revenue from affiliate marketing.

Benefits of Passive Income

1. Financial Freedom: It allows you to break free from the conventional 9-5 job, providing a pathway to attain financial independence sooner.

2. Diversified Earnings: Passive income serves as a financial safety net. In case one source diminishes, others are available to compensate.

3. Flexibility: The earnings are not tied to a specific number of hours worked, offering you the flexibility to pursue other interests and passions.

4. Financial Growth: Certain sources of passive income, like investments, tend to appreciate over time, providing both income and capital gains.

5. Reduced Stress: With a stable passive income, there is generally less stress about meeting financial obligations.

6. Opportunity for Exploration: A steady passive income stream provides the chance to explore new business opportunities and passions without financial constraint.

Common Myths and Misconceptions

1. "Passive Income Requires No Work": Although passive income eventually requires minimal effort, significant initial input, commitment, and sometimes capital is often necessary.

2. "It's Effortless Money": Establishing a reliable source of passive income is often challenging and requires a well-thought-out strategy and dedication.

3. "Passive Income is for the Wealthy": While capital can be beneficial, several passive income streams, like blogging or affiliate marketing, require more time and effort than substantial financial investment.

4. "All Passive Income Streams are Identical": Different passive income sources come with varying levels of risk, effort, and return on investment.

5. "Passive Income is Set-and-Forget": Most passive income streams require occasional oversight, updating, and management to remain viable and profitable.

Conclusion

Grasping the concept of passive income is essential for anyone looking to start a home business. Though it isn't a fast track to wealth, with careful planning and commitment, passive income can significantly contribute to your financial independence. In the next step, we'll explore how to identify and select the right niche to kickstart your passive income journey.

This step should offer readers a solid foundation to understand passive income, preparing them for the subsequent steps in establishing a home-based business dedicated to generating passive income.

Step 2: Identifying Your Niche

Introduction

Selecting the right niche is pivotal for the success of your home-based passive income venture. This step helps you navigate through the process of niche selection by exploring various options, aligning them with your personal strengths and interests, and finally, validating your niche choice to ensure its profitability and sustainability.

Exploring Different Niches

To start, familiarize yourself with the myriad of niches available. Different niches present unique opportunities for passive income, and your task is to find one that resonates with you. Here's a brief overview:

1. **Real Estate Investment:** Engage in buying or renting properties.

2. **Dividend Stocks:** Invest in dividend-yielding stocks.

3. **Affiliate Marketing:** Promote products for a commission.

4. **Online Course Creation:** Leverage your knowledge and create educational content.

5. **E-Book Writing:** Author and publish digital books.

6. **App Development:** Develop and monetize mobile applications.

7. **Print on Demand:** Design and sell custom products.

Consider factors like market demand, competition level, potential profitability, and the required learning curve for each niche.

Matching Niche to Your Skills and Interests

Selecting a niche that aligns with your skills and interests is crucial. This congruence ensures enduring motivation and enthusiasm in your venture:

- **Skills Inventory:** Enumerate your competencies and areas of expertise.
- **Passion Identification:** Recognize areas you are passionate about.
- **Niche Alignment:** Find the overlap between profitable niches and your skills and passions.

Validating Your Niche Choice

Validation is the final yet essential step to confirm the practicality and potential success of your chosen niche.

- **Market Analysis:** Conduct thorough research to understand the niche's demand and competition using tools and platforms dedicated to market analytics.
- **Customer Profiling:** Clearly define your target audience, understanding their needs, behaviors, and preferences.
- **Pilot Testing:** Launch a small-scale, low-risk version of your offering to collect feedback and gauge market interest.

Conclusion

Selecting and validating a niche is a fundamental step towards building a thriving home business focused on passive income. It requires a deep dive into various niche options, an honest assessment of your skills and interests, and validation of market demand for your offerings. With a clear niche identified, you're ready to advance to crafting a robust business plan in the next step.

Through meticulous niche identification and validation, you set the stage for a successful and fulfilling passive income venture, poised for sustainable success and growth.

Step 3: Crafting Your Business Plan

Introduction

A strategic business plan acts as a compass for your passive income venture, delineating your path with clarity and focus. It's not merely a document but a structured reflection of your vision, goals, and strategy for success.

Why Planning Matters

Planning is not just a preliminary phase but a crucial foundation for your business:

1. Clarifying Vision: The planning process helps refine and articulate your business idea, providing a clear vision and direction.

2. Risk Reduction: Identifying and addressing potential challenges and risks early on ensures a smoother entrepreneurial journey.

3. Efficient Resource Allocation: Through meticulous planning, efficiently deploy your resources, maximizing your efforts and investment.

4. Attracting Investors: A coherent and persuasive business plan is essential if you intend to seek external funding.

Establishing Goals and Objectives

Setting well-defined goals and objectives offers a roadmap for your business activities:

- **SMART Framework:** Formulate goals that are Specific, Measurable, Achievable, Relevant, and Time-bound.
- **Immediate Objectives:** Define your short-term targets and what you intend to accomplish in the initial phases.
- **Future Aspirations:** Develop a vision for your business's long-term future and the milestones you aim to achieve.

- **Milestone Planning:** Segment your goals into manageable and achievable milestones for systematic progression.

Drafting Your Business Plan

Your business plan should be concise yet comprehensive. Below is a simplified structure to guide your drafting process:

1. Executive Summary: A brief overview of your business, encapsulating the mission, vision, and founding date.

2. Business Description: A deeper insight into your business, highlighting the problems it addresses and the solutions it provides.

3. Market Analysis: A study of the market dynamics, your target demographic, and the competitive environment.

4. Organizational Structure: An illustration of your business's hierarchy and introduction to key personnel.

5. Product/Service Line: An exposition of your offerings, with details on pricing and value proposition.

6. Marketing Strategy: A plan detailing how you intend to promote your offerings to your target audience.

7. Funding Request (if needed): A section dedicated to outlining your funding requirements and utilization plan.

8. Financial Projections: A forecast of your financial trajectory, including expected revenue, costs, and profit margins.

9. Appendix: Supplement your plan with additional supporting documents, charts, or graphs as necessary.

Conclusion

Constructing a business plan may seem like a daunting task, but its value is immeasurable. With a structured plan, you not only visualize your business's success but also chart a course to achieve it. This plan will be your guiding star as you proceed to bring your passive income business to life, steering you confidently through the challenges and triumphs ahead.

Remember, a well-orchestrated plan is the first step towards transforming your passive income dreams into a tangible and successful reality.

Step 4: Setting Up Your Home Business

Introduction

Upon establishing a business plan and choosing a niche, the next logical step is to officially set up your home business. This phase involves making crucial decisions regarding the business structure, complying with legal requirements, and creating an efficient home office setup conducive to productivity and success.

Selecting Business Structure

The structure you select for your business profoundly impacts your operations, taxes, and how much personal liability you incur. Familiarize yourself with the common types:

1. Sole Proprietorship: Ideal for solo entrepreneurs, it's easy to set up but comes with personal liability for business debts.

2. Partnership: Suitable for businesses with multiple owners, distributing responsibility and liability among partners.

3. Limited Liability Company (LLC): Offers liability protection with tax benefits but involves more paperwork.

4. Corporation: Provides the most liability protection, yet it's complex and costly to maintain.

Choose a structure that aligns with your business size, future goals, and the level of liability you're willing to assume.

Registration and Legal Requirements

Legal compliance is non-negotiable, ensuring your business operates within the bounds of the law:

- **Business Name Registration:** Your business name must be unique and registered, often through your state's Secretary of State office.
- **Employer Identification Number (EIN):** Obtain an EIN from the IRS for tax purposes, even if you don't plan to

have employees.

- **Business Licenses and Permits:** Acquire the necessary licenses and permits applicable to your niche and local jurisdiction.
- **Zoning Laws:** Understand and comply with local zoning laws, especially if you're operating from a residential area.

Setting Up Your Home Office

Creating a designated workspace at home is essential for focus and productivity:

- **Dedicated Space:** Choose a quiet, comfortable space minimally exposed to household distractions.
- **Ergonomic Furniture:** Invest in ergonomic chairs and desks to facilitate long hours of work comfortably and healthily.
- **Technology:** Ensure you have reliable internet connectivity, a functional computer, and necessary software and applications for your business operations.
- **Storage:** Organize your space with adequate storage solutions to keep your work area tidy and documents easily accessible.
- **Lighting:** Natural light is ideal, but also invest in quality artificial lighting to reduce eye strain.

Conclusion

Setting up your home business involves meticulous attention to legal details and creating an environment that supports sustained productivity and business growth. With the right structure, legal compliance, and a conducive workspace, you're laying a solid foundation for your home business to thrive in the competitive market. As you progress, the subsequent steps will guide you through launching your first product or service and scaling your business to new heights.

By attentively navigating through these initial setup stages, you're not only legitimizing your business but also crafting a workspace that will serve as the launchpad for all your future entrepreneurial successes.

Step 5: Unveiling Your First Product/Service

Introduction

With the foundational aspects of your business in place, the stage is set for the launch of your initial product or service. This integral step encompasses the fine-tuning of your offering, the formulation of a sensible pricing strategy, and the deployment of compelling launch and promotional maneuvers.

Product Development

Crafting a noteworthy product or service necessitates a careful, detail-oriented process:

1. Market Analysis: Begin with in-depth research to discern the requirements and desires of potential customers, shaping a product or service that adeptly addresses these needs.

2. Quality Assurance: Prioritize excellence, possibly engaging in beta testing or pilot services to garner constructive feedback for refinements pre-launch.

3. Distinctive Branding: Forge a recognizable brand, incorporating an appealing name, logo, and design elements that captivate your target market.

4. Streamlined Supply Chain (if applicable): Establish dependable procedures for the manufacturing and distribution of physical products to ensure prompt and efficient delivery.

Pricing Strategies

Constructing a sensible pricing model involves balancing costs, value perception, and profitability:

1. Cost-Based Approach: Tally the entirety of production costs, appending a profit margin to derive your selling price.

2. Value-Oriented Approach: Determine your price based on the perceived worth of your product or service to consumers.

3. Competitor Insight: Examine pricing structures of competing products, strategically positioning yours within the prevailing market context.

4. Psychological Pricing Techniques: Implement pricing formats that subtly encourage purchases, like pricing items slightly below a rounded number.

Launch and Promotion Strategies

Effective promotion is instrumental to a successful launch:

1. Pre-Launch Buzz: Engage potential customers with sneak peeks, email campaigns, and partnerships with influencers to generate excitement and anticipation.

2. Introductory Offers: Introduce special deals, discounts, or exclusives for early adopters to stimulate initial sales and garner reviews.

3. Social Media Engagement: Actively utilize social platforms to reach and engage your audience, disseminating compelling content related to your launch.

4. Email Campaigns: Cultivate and segment your mailing list for tailored promotional communications.

5. Public Relations Efforts: Draft press releases, collaborate with media partners, or host launch events to spotlight your new product or service.

Conclusion

The launch of your first offering marks a significant juncture in your entrepreneurial adventure. A meticulously crafted, appropriately priced product, bolstered by a well-strategized launch, lays a robust foundation for sustained business growth and success. Remain agile and responsive to consumer feedback and market shifts, refining your approach as necessary to resonate with your audience and meet market demand effectively.

The exhilaration of a product launch is a unique experience, combining anticipation with the satisfaction of seeing your plans come to fruition. With a thoughtful approach and strategic planning, this step forward is not just exciting but also a concrete move towards carving your niche in the market and establishing a reliable source of passive income.

Step 6: Automating And Scaling

Introduction

Post the launch of your initial offering, the next pivotal phase involves sustaining and broadening your business's horizons. Automation and scaling are imperative to fostering the growth of your passive income, necessitating adept utilization of technology, including Artificial Intelligence (AI), effective outsourcing, and strategic scaling approaches.

Utilizing Technology and Tools

Technology is a valuable ally in making your business operations more efficient:

1. Automation Software: Invest in applications that facilitate the automation of routine tasks such as scheduling, billing, and social media updates, allowing you more time for strategic endeavors.

2. Customer Relationship Management (CRM): Adopt CRM systems to meticulously organize and manage customer interactions and enhance your sales initiatives.

3. E-commerce Solutions: If your business entails product sales, select e-commerce platforms providing comprehensive tools for sales, shipping, and customer service.

4. Email Marketing Platforms: Sophisticated tools are available to automate email communications, offering features like scheduling, list segmentation, and performance tracking.

5. Artificial Intelligence (AI): Implement AI technologies for tasks like customer service through chatbots, data analysis for market trends, and personalized product recommendations for customers. AI can significantly streamline operations and provide valuable insights to drive your business's growth.

Outsourcing Tasks

Outsourcing becomes indispensable as your business expands:

1. Virtual Assistants: Employ virtual assistants to undertake administrative duties, handle customer inquiries, or manage your social media presence.

2. Freelancers: Engage freelance professionals for specialized or short-term projects, including graphic design, content generation, or strategic marketing planning.

3. Third-party Services: Consider enlisting external services specializing in areas like accounting, legal advice, or IT support, ensuring these critical functions are handled with expertise.

Strategies for Scaling Your Business

Intelligent scaling is vital for the sustainable growth of your business:

1. Diversification: Broaden your portfolio by introducing new products or services, reaching diverse customer segments and creating multiple income streams.

2. Market Expansion: Explore and penetrate new market segments or geographical locations, expanding your customer reach and sales potential.

3. Strategic Partnerships: Forge alliances with other businesses, influencers, or brands to tap into their established audiences and bolster your market visibility.

4. Customer Retention Initiatives: Implement strategies like loyalty programs, stellar customer service, and active community engagement to retain current customers and foster repeat business.

Conclusion

The processes of automation and scaling are integral to strengthening and enlarging your passive income avenues. By incorporating technology, including AI, engaging in strategic outsourcing, and applying mindful scaling strategies, you pave the way for increased revenue and a structured business model that supports continual growth and success. With these mechanisms activated, your enterprise is better equipped to meet the challenges of growth while seizing the abundant opportunities it presents.

Through automation, including the use of AI, and a well-devised scaling strategy, your passive income venture is not only positioned for growth but also streamlined for efficient operation, allowing you to relish and manage the rewards of your hard work more effortlessly and enjoyably.

Step 7: Managing Finances And Taxes

Introduction

A thriving home business requires not only generating income but also effectively managing finances and navigating through taxes. This final step guides you through basic accounting principles, ensuring tax compliance, and sharing invaluable tips for prudent financial management.

Basic Accounting Principles

Understanding and applying basic accounting principles is fundamental for tracking and managing your business finances:

1. Double-Entry Bookkeeping: Each financial transaction affects at least two accounts, ensuring the accounting equation stays balanced: Assets = Liabilities + Equity.

2. Accrual Accounting: Record revenues and expenses when they are earned or incurred, regardless of when the cash is received or paid.

3. Financial Statements Understanding: Familiarize yourself with essential statements like the income statement, balance sheet, and cash flow statement, each providing different financial insights.

Tax Planning and Compliance

Being proactive about tax planning and compliance is vital to avoid legal issues and optimize your tax position:

1. Understand Tax Obligations: Different business structures have varied tax obligations. Know what taxes your business is liable for, including income, self-employment, sales, and property taxes.

2. Keep Accurate Records: Maintain detailed and accurate records of all income, expenses, and tax deductions to make tax filing smoother and ensure you're not overpaying taxes.

3. Seek Professional Advice: Consider consulting with a tax advisor or accountant who can guide you on tax planning, compliance, and potential deductions and credits you might qualify for.

Financial Management Tips

Adopting sound financial management practices is crucial for the longevity and success of your business:

1. Emergency Fund: Establish a reserve of funds to cover unexpected expenses or financial downturns, providing a safety net for your business.

2. Budgeting: Develop and adhere to a budget, outlining expected revenues and expenses, helping you make informed financial decisions and maintain profitability.

3. Regular Financial Review: Conduct periodic reviews of your financial statements to monitor your business's financial health and identify areas for improvement or adjustment.

4. Invest in Growth: Allocate resources for business development and growth initiatives, like marketing, product development, or employee training.

Conclusion

Effective financial and tax management is the cornerstone of a successful and sustainable home business. By mastering basic accounting principles, staying compliant with tax obligations, and implementing smart financial management practices, you set your business up for stability and growth. With these financial foundations in place, you are well-equipped to enjoy the rewards of your entrepreneurial efforts and see your passive income streams flourish.

Armed with sound financial knowledge and strategies, your

passive income business is not just poised for survival but destined for success. This financial acumen will not only protect your venture but also fuel its growth, ensuring a stable and prosperous entrepreneurial journey ahead.

Conclusion

As we wrap up this guide, let's briefly revisit the pivotal steps on your journey to starting a home business:

1. **Understanding Passive Income:** Recognizing the value of earning with less active involvement, and dispelling misconceptions.

2. **Identifying Your Niche:** Aligning business ideas with your passions and skills.

3. **Creating a Business Plan:** Drafting a blueprint for your business's direction and growth.

4. **Setting Up Your Home Business:** Laying the foundational structures and ensuring legal compliance.

5. **Launching Your First Product/Service:** Bringing your vision to fruition with a strong market presence.

6. **Automating and Scaling:** Streamlining operations and expanding horizons, including embracing AI technology.

7. **Managing Finances and Taxes:** Ensuring financial health through prudent management and tax compliance.

The path to building a passive income from a home business is both exhilarating and challenging. But with the steps outlined in this guide, you're not navigating the terrain blindfolded; you have a map, a compass, and the tools you need.

Final Tips and Advice

- **Stay Adaptable:** The business landscape is ever-evolving. Be ready to pivot or make changes as needed.
- **Never Stop Learning:** Whether it's about your niche, technology, or business strategies, continuous learning is the key to staying ahead.
- **Network:** Connect with fellow entrepreneurs and

potential customers. Their insights can be invaluable.
- **Listen to Feedback:** Customer feedback is a goldmine. Use it to improve and innovate.

Embrace the adventure ahead with enthusiasm and determination. Your vision, combined with the strategies in this guide, will steer you towards a fulfilling and successful entrepreneurial journey.

www.ingramcontent.com/pod-product-compliance
Lightning Source LLC
Chambersburg PA
CBHW072229290526
45794CB00007B/2954